Diet recommendations for TCM - Liver - wind

Please check these recommendations always with a nutrition consultant, therapist, doctor or dietician. The recipes and the list of ingredients are supporting the conventional medical therapy.
The calorie disclosures of fresh ingredients (fruit and vegetables) vary according to quality and time of harvest. The contents were checked by a dietician and a nutrition consultant for the Traditional Chinese Medicine (TCM).

Author:
©2019 Josef Miligui
www.ebns.at

AF190381

Source:
The lists are created from the EBNS database for nutritional counseling. The database is used by dietitians, therapists and doctors for advising the patient / client.

Literature:
The specialist literature and the training documents of the German and Austrian dietary and traditional Chinese medicine serve as a knowledge base. We have used the documents as a basis of knowledge, adapted it to our experience and completed them.
http://di-book.com

Production and publishing:
BoD – Books on Demand, Norderstedt
ISBN: 9783746089164

Diet recommendations for TCM - Liver - wind

1   Treatment strategy

Divert wind, cool heat (see liver fire), lower yang (see ascending liver yang), nourish blood and yin (see
liver blood deficiency)

2   Avoid

Yangisier cooking methods, eggs, crabmeat, oats, alcohol, hot spices, chicken.

3   Breakfast

	kkal. per serving
Champignon rice	410
Creamy potatoes with cauliflower	332
Fennel-Rice Soup	155
Grated carrots with apple	74
Polenta with ratatouille	225
Rice congee with honey pear and black sesame	158
Roasted millet with Celery sticks	400
Roasted nuts	973
Rucola salad with tomatoes	129
Tea from coriander	2

4   Snack

5   Lunch

6   Afternoon

7 Dinner

8 Any time

9 Recipes

(rec.) = You can use more.
(little) = You should use less than specified
(omit) = omit.

9.1 Basic recipe for a chicken broth worming

Strengthens Qi and blood, is very warm.
Cooking time approx. 2-3 hours
Calories p. portion: 90
9 portions
Allergens: L

Quantity of ingredients:
Chicken meat 1/2 piece / 600g. (rec.) - warm - sweet .... wood
Carrot 2 pieces / 150g. (yes) - neutral - sweet ....earth
Leek 1 stick / 45g. (little) - warm - acrid... metal
Celery root 1 piece / 500g. (rec.) - cool - sweet..earth
Ginger fresh 2 slices / 2g. (little) - warm - acrid .... metal
Juniper berry 1 teaspoon / 3g. (omit) - warm - sweet, acrid, bitter ....fire
Bay leaf 3 pieces / 2g. (little) - warm - acrid .... metal
Water 4 cup / 900g. (yes) - cool - salty..earth

Cooking instructions:
Remove chicken parts from fat. Place chicken pieces in a saucepan
with hot water and heat till it boils briefly, skimming any resulting foam.
Add coarsely chopped vegetables and all spices and cook over medium
heat for 2 to 3 hours. Strain the finished soup. Throw away vegetables
and bones.
Tip: If you want to use the meat as a soup insert, take out after 45
minutes and return only the bones in the soup.
Refrigerate for later use.

9.2 Basic recipe for a reissue soup (Congee)

Warms the stomach and spleen, harmonizes the intestine, forces Qi,
reduces moisture.
Cooking time approx. 2-4 hours
Calories p. portion: 140
3 portions

Quantity of ingredients:
Rice variety any 1 cup / 120g. (yes) - warm - sweet................................. metal
Water 6 cups / 700g. (yes) - cool - salty ....earth

Cooking instructions:
Cook rice and water in a ratio of about 1: 6. The amount of water determines the thickness of the mash (matter of taste).
Put the rice in a saucepan with a heavy lid. It is important to simmer the rice after a short boil on the slightest flame, otherwise it burns.
Boil the rice for 2-4 hours. The longer it cooks, the more it strengthens. If you want to eat the dish for breakfast, you can put the rice on just before bedtime.
To be on the safe side, you should first check the behavior of your pot and cooker under observation for a similar amount of time, so that nothing burns.
Refrigerate for later use.

9.3   Basic recipe for a vegetable soup, nutritious

Strengthens spleen and lung, regulates Qi flow, builds up Qi, dries out, passes downwardly, strengthens stomach Qi.
Cooking time approx. 2-3 hours
Calories p. portion: 48
5 portions
Allergens: L

Quantity of ingredients:
Olive oil 1 table spoon / 4g. (little) - cool - sweet ....earth
Onion white 1 piece / 60g. (little) - warm - acrid ....metal
Carrot 3 pieces / 200g. (yes) - neutral - sweet ....earth
Parsnip 3/8 lbs - 6oz / 150g. (yes) - cool - bitter..fire
Celery root 1 cup / 100g. (rec.) - cool - sweet ....earth
Ginger fresh 1/2 teaspoon / 2g. (little) - warm - acrid ....metal
Lemon 1/2 piece / 25g. (rec.) - cold - sour..wood
Juniper berry 6 pieces / 6g. (omit) - warm - sweet, acrid, bitter....................fire
Thyme dried 1 pinch / 1g. (omit) - warm - bitter..metal
Lovage 1 table spoon / 3g. (omit) - warm - acrid, bitter ....metal
Bay leaf 2 leaves / 1g. (little) - warm - acrid ....metal
Salt 1 pinch / 1g. (little) - cold - salty ....water
Water 3 cups / 650g. (yes) - cool - salty ....earth

Cooking instructions:
Cut the vegetables into cubes.
Heat oil in hot pot, fry shortly onions and vegetables.
Add cold water, then add ginger, bay leaf and lemon juice.
Season with juniper, thyme and lovage. Cover for 2 - 3 hours on a low heat and simmer.
The used vegetables should be thrown away.

The basic recipe serves as a soup base and to refine vegetables, legumes or cereals.
If you want to eat vegetable soup immediately, add the desired vegetables half an hour before.
Refrigerate for later use.

9.4   Broccoli cream soup

Nourishes lung Yin, produces humors, strengthens spleen and liver, moisturizes, reduces cold-evil, softens knots.
Cooking time approx. 30 min
Calories p. portion: 98
6 portions
Allergens: LO

Quantity of ingredients:
Olive oil 2 table spoons / 7g. (little) - cool - sweet ....earth
Broccoli 1,1 lbs / 500g. (yes) - cool - sweet...earth
Carrot 2 pieces / 150g. (yes) - neutral - sweet ....earth
Potato 2 pieces / 120g. (yes) - neutral - sweet...earth
Onion white 1 piece / 50g. (little) - warm - acrid .... metal
Water 1 cup / 50g. (yes) - cool - salty...earth
Basic recipe for a vegetable soup (nutritious) 2 cup / 500g. (yes) - neutral - *. *
White wine 1/2 cup / 125g. (yes) - cool - sweet, bitter, acrid .... wood
Sage 1 teaspoon / 2g. (yes) - cool - bitter, spicy ....fire
Rosemary 1 teaspoon / 2g. (little) - warm - bitter ....fire
Pepper (ground) 1 pinch / 0,5g. () - warm - acrid .... metal
Salt 1 pinch / 1g. (little) - cold - salty .... water

Cooking instructions:
Add the olive oil to the pan, add the washed and cut broccoli, diced carrots and potatoes, sauté for a short time, add the chopped onion, fill with water, enough water to cover the vegetables at least 3 finger breadths. Add bouillon, salt, add a little bit of white wine, add the seasoned sage and rosemary.
Heat till it boils and then simmer on a small fire for about 25 minutes.
Season with pepper, if necessary season with sea salt. Purée the soup.

9.5 Celery and tomato salad

Nourishes liver-Yin, produces humors, brings the liver Qi in motion, cools heat, relaxes, builds up Qi.
Cooking time approx. 10 min
Calories p. portion: 245
1 portion
Allergens: GHL

Quantity of ingredients:

Celery sticks 3-4 twigs / 50g. (yes) - cool - sweet ....earth
Tomato 4 pieces / 200g. (rec.) - cold - sweet-sour ....wood
Basil 3 leaves (fresh) / 1g. (yes) - warm - acrid, bitter..................................fire
Yogurt (natural, 1.5% fat) 3 table spoons / 30g. (omit) - cool - sour .... wood
Olive oil 1/2 teaspoon / 5g. (little) - cool - sweet..earth
Lemon juice 1 table spoon / 10g. (rec.) - cold - sour .... wood
Salt 1 pinch / 0,5g. (little) - cold - salty ....water
Sugar white 1 pinch / 0,5g. (omit) - cold - sweet ....earth
Pepper (ground) 1 pinch / 0,2g. () - warm - acrid ....metal
Hazelnuts 2 table spoons / 20g. (rec.) - neutral - sweet ....earth

Cooking instructions:

Clean celery, possibly remove threads and cut into fine rings. Wash tomatoes and dice. For the sauce, mix yoghurt with olive oil and lemon juice and season with the spices. Add the prepared tomatoes and celery to the sauce and mix. Finely chop whole hazelnuts or sprinkle ground hazelnuts over the fresh food and serve the salad garnished with basil leaves.

9.6 Champignon rice

Strengthens spleen, builds up Qi, directs heat down, strengthens stomach Qi, cools blood heat.
Cooking time approx. 30 min
Calories p. portion: 410
2 portions
Allergens: L

Quantity of ingredients:

Onion white 1 piece / 50g. (little) - warm - acrid ....metal
Bay leaf 2 pieces / 1g. (little) - warm - acrid ....metal
Clove 2 pieces / 1g. (little) - warm - acrid ....metal
Basic recipe for a vegetable soup (nutritious) 7/8 lbs / 350g. (yes) - neutral - **
Rice (whole grain) 5/8 oz / 200g. (yes) - warm - sweet ....metal
Champignon 1/8 lbs - 2oz / 60g. (yes) - cool - sweet ....earth

Parsley 1/2 oz / 20g. (rec.) - warm - bitter .... wood
Pepper (ground) 1 pinch / 0,2g. () - warm - acrid .... metal

Cooking instructions:
Plug in the cloves in the onion. Heat the vegetable stock with the onion and the bay leaves till it boils. Add the rice to the boiling liquid, reduce the temperature to the lowest level and stir with the lid closed for 20-25 minutes.
In the meantime, wash the mushrooms, clean them, slice them, sauté briefly with a little water or sauté. Wash the parsley and chop finely. Remove the onion from the rice, add the mushrooms and the parsley, season with pepper.

9.7 Chicken soup with angelica root and buckthorn fruit

Strengthens spleen and nourishes the blood and Yin of the liver, forces Qi and blood, is very warming.
Cooking time approx. 1 1/2 hours
Calories p. portion: 77
3 portions
Allergens: LO

Quantity of ingredients:
Basic recipe for a chicken soup (warming) 2 cup / 500g. (rec.) - warm - * .... *
Bocksdorn fruits (Lycii, goji berry dried 1/8 lbs - 2oz / 50g. (yes) - cool - . wood

Cooking instructions:
When you cook chicken broth according to basic recipes add angelica root and willowberry fruits in the last 40 minutes.

Ingestion: Drink 2-3 cups of broth daily.

9.8 Chicken soup with egg yolk and parsley

Forces Qi and blood, is very warming, nourishes blood and liver, harmonizes liver and spleen, forces eyesight, preserves the fluids, contracts.
Cooking time approx. 10 min
Calories p. portion: 118
2 portions
Allergens: CL

Quantity of ingredients:
Basic recipe for a chicken soup (warming) 2 cup / 500g. (rec.) - warm - * .... *
Chicken yolk 1 piece / 10g. (rec.) - neutral - sweet .... earth
Parsley 1 table spoon / 10g. (rec.) - warm - bitter .... wood

Cooking instructions:
Cook the chicken broth according to the basic recipe.
Heat broth and bubble the egg yolk. Sprinkle the chopped parsley over it and let it rest for about 2 minutes. Drink in small sips.

9.9   Creamy potatoes with cauliflower

Forces Qi, forces spleen, relieves inflammation, moisturizes, relaxes, builds up Qi, spreads, nourishes lung Yin, produces humors, cools inner heat, strengthens Qi and kidney Jing, harmonizes liver and spleen, forces eyesight.
Cooking time approx. 30 min
Calories p. portion: 332
1 portion
Allergens: CG

Quantity of ingredients:
Potato 3/8 lbs - 6oz / 150g. (yes) - neutral - sweet .... earth
Cauliflower 1/8 lbs - 2oz / 50g. (yes) - cool - sweet .... earth
Cow's milk (3.5% fat) 3 table spoons / 30g. (yes) - neutral - sweet .... earth
Cream, sweet 30% 1 table spoon / 10g. (little) - neutral - sweet .... earth
Butter organic 1 teaspoon / 10g. (yes) - neutral - sweet .... earth
Parsley 1 teaspoon / 3g. (rec.) - warm - bitter .... wood
Chicken yolk 1 piece / 25g. (rec.) - neutral - sweet .... earth

Cooking instructions:
Wash the potatoes under running water, thoroughly wash the cauliflower in stagnant water.
Divide the cauliflower florets into small buds, cut the stems into pieces about 1 cm in size.
Peel the potatoes and cut into 2 cm cubes.
Heat the milk with the cream in a saucepan, add the potatoes and the cauliflower. Cook on low heat for about 15 minutes.
Put the vegetables in a plate, add the butter, the chopped parsley and the egg yolk and lightly knead and mix everything with a fork.

9.10 Fennel-Rice Soup

Regulates Qi, warms the inside, lowers cold, forces stomach, relieves constipation, forces Yang, dissolves mucus, reduces wind, spreads, strengthens Qi and kidney Jing, builds up Qi.
Cooking time approx. 15-20 min
Calories p. portion: 156
2 portions
Allergens: EG

Quantity of ingredients:
Basic recipe for a rice soup (Congee) 1 cup / 300g. (yes) - neutral - sweet..... *
Fennel 1/2 piece / 150g. (yes) - warm - sweet, little acrid .... earth
Butter organic 1 table spoon / 15g. (yes) - neutral - sweet .... earth
Soy sauce 1 dash / 3g. (little) - cold - salty .... water

Cooking instructions:
Cook the fennel softly in the rice soup according to the basic recipe.
Before serving, add a piece of butter and some soy sauce.

9.11 Grated carrots with apple

Strengthens spleen and liver, regulates Qi flow, moisturizes, relaxes, builds up Qi, spreads, nourishes fluids, reduces stomach heat, forces spleen, produces essence, harmonizes stomach, cools heat, preserves the fluids, contracts.
Cooking time approx. 10 min
Calories p. portion: 74
1 portion

Quantity of ingredients:
Carrot 10 cups / 100g. (yes) - neutral - sweet .... earth
Apple (sweet) 1 piece / 50g. (yes) - cool - sweet, sour .... earth
Lemon juice 2 teaspoons / 3g. (rec.) - cold - sour .... wood
Sugar substitute (sweetener) 1g. Or 0,034oz / 1g. (yes) - cool - sweet .... *

Cooking instructions:
Mix lemon juice with sweetener. Grate the washed, thinly peeled carrots and the apple piece into the sauce and mix.

9.12 Grilled tomatoes with cheese filling

Nourishes liver-Yin, cools heat, produces humors, gets Qi moving, reduces internal heat, dries out, passes downwardly, preserves the fluids.
Cooking time approx. 30 min
Calories p. portion: 470
2 portions
Allergens: ACG

Quantity of ingredients:
Tomato 8 pieces / 200g. (rec.) - cold - sweet-sour .... wood
Feta cheese 0,2 lbs / 75g. (omit) - warm - bitter..fire
Fresh cheese 0,2 lbs / 75g. (little) - cool - sour .... wood
Chicken egg 1 piece / 60g. (little) - neutral - sweet ....earth
Olive oil 1 table spoon / 12g. (little) - cool - sweet.....................................earth
Basil (fresh) 1 table spoon / 6g. (omit) - warm - acrid, bitter..................... metal
Basil (fresh) 1 table spoon / 6g. (omit) - warm - acrid, bitter..................... metal
Salt 1 pinch / 1g. (little) - cold - salty .... water
Pepper (ground) 1 pinch / 0,5g. () - warm - acrid .... metal
Olives 1 oz / 30g. (yes) - neutral - sweet, rough...fire
Rucola 1/4 lbs / 100g. () - cool - acrid...fire
White bread (wheat bread) 4 slices / 80g. (yes) - cool - sweet................. wood

Cooking instructions:
Hollow out tomatoes generously. Put in a casserole dish.
Mix cheese, olive oil, egg, chopped basil and flour. Season with salt and pepper and fill in the tomatoes.
Bake in the preheated oven at 210 degrees on the middle rail for 15 minutes, then switch on the oven grill and grill for a further 3 minutes (without circulating air).
Stone the olives and chop and sprinkle on the tomatoes.
Garnish tomatoes with rocket and serve with white bread.

9.13 Italian Vegetable and Bean Soup

Moisturizes skin, diuretic, strengthens stomach Qi, moisturizes, relaxes, builds up Qi, nourishes liver-Yin, cools heat, produces humors, strengthens spleen and liver, regulates Qi flow, moisturizes, relaxes, builds up Qi, spreads.
Cooking time approx. 1 hour
Calories p. portion: 204
4 portions
Allergens: L

Quantity of ingredients:

Butter beans white 5/8 oz / 200g. (yes) - neutral - sweet .... water
Onion (shallot) 1 piece / 20g. (little) - warm - acrid, sweet........................ metal
Carrot 1 piece / 70g. (yes) - neutral - sweet ....earth
Olive oil 2 table spoons / 20g. (little) - cool - sweet ....earth
Tomato 2 pieces / 80g. (rec.) - cold - sweet-sour .... wood
Celery root 1/4 lbs / 100g. (rec.) - cool - sweet...earth
White cabbage 0,2 lbs / 70g. (yes) - neutral - sweet ....earth
Endive salad 1/8 lbs - 2oz / 50g. (little) - neutral - bitter ....fire
Salt 1 pinch / 1g. (little) - cold - salty .... water
Pepper (ground) 1 pinch / 0,2g. () - warm - acrid .... metal
Water 2 cup / 450g. (yes) - cool - salty..earth

Cooking instructions:

Soak beans and cook for 1/2 hour.
Fry onions, carrots and celery in frying oil.
Add tomatoes and water and simmer for 30 minutes.
Cut white cabbage into strips. Add the cabbage and endive salad and
the boiled beans, and season with salt, pepper and olive oil.

9.14 Lettuce with fresh cheese

Forces heart and kidneys Yin.
Cooking time approx. 5 min
Calories p. portion: 498
1 portion
Allergens: AFM

Quantity of ingredients:

Leaf salads (bitter) 2 portions / 60g. (rec.) - neutral - sweet, bitter ....fire
Lemon juice 1 dash / 3g. (rec.) - cold - sour... wood
Salt 1 pinch / 1g. (little) - cold - salty .... water
Pepper (ground) 1 pinch / 0,5g. () - warm - acrid .... metal
Black caraway 1 pinch / 1g. (little) - warm - acrid, sweet................................ *

Cooking instructions:

Wash lettuce and finely pluck.
Mix 150 ml cream cheese, splashes of mustard, splashes of lemon
juice, 1 clove of garlic, chopped fresh herbs, pinch of pepper and
crushed black cumin and pour over. Serve with wholemeal bread.

9.15 Minestrone

Forces Qi of the middle, cools heat, diuretic, cools blood, reduces mucus, reduces heat, moisturizes, relaxes, builds up Qi, spreads. nourishes liver-Yin, cools heat, produces humors.
Cooking time approx. 30 min
Calories p. portion: 211
4 portions
Allergens: GL

Quantity of ingredients:

Onion (shallot) 2 pieces / 40g. (little) - warm - acrid, sweet.......................metal
Sunflower oil 1 teaspoon / 10g. (little) - cool - sweet ....earth
Water 2 cup / 480g. (yes) - cool - salty...earth
Carrot 2 pieces / 120g. (yes) - neutral - sweet ....earth
Savoy cabbage / kale 1 handful / 15g. (yes) - neutral - sweet...................earth
Beans (green, fresh) 1 handful / 20g. (yes) - neutral - sweet ....water
Celery sticks 3 pieces / 20g. (yes) - cool - sweet ....earth
Peas, green 4 table spoons / 30g. (yes) - neutral - sweet ....water
Zucchini 1 piece / 200g. (yes) - cool - sweet ....earth
Rice variety any 1 cup / 120g. (yes) - warm - sweet...................................metal
Bay leaf 3 leaves / 1g. (little) - warm - acrid ....metal
Sunflower oil 1 table spoon / 10g. (little) - cool - sweet ....earth
Salt 1 pinch / 1g. (little) - cold - salty ....water
Tomato 3 pieces / 150g. (rec.) - cold - sweet-sour ....wood
Thyme 1 Twig / 3g. (little) - warm - bitter...*
Basil 4 leaves / 2g. (yes) - warm - acrid, bitter ....fire

Cooking instructions:

Fry the onion in oil in a glassy saucepan and add water. Add vegetables, rice and salt and simmer gently. If the vegetables are firm, add tomatoes, a small sprig of thyme, basil and bay leaf and leave to simmer. Serve with Parmesan.

9.16 Polenta with ratatouille

Strengthens stomach Qi, diuretic, moisturizes, relaxes, builds up Qi, spreads, nourishes liver-Yin, cools heat, produces humors, cools and moves blood, reduces external and internal wind, reduces internal heat.
Cooking time approx. 30 min
Calories p. portion: 226
4 portions
Allergens: G

Quantity of ingredients:

Corn Grease (Polenta) 1 cup / 120g. (yes) - neutral - sweet ....earth
Water 1 1/2 cups / 240g. (yes) - cool - salty..earth
Aubergine 1 piece (large) / 200g. (rec.) - cool - sweet ....earth
Zucchini 2 pieces / 500g. (yes) - cool - sweet ....earth
Onion white 2 pieces / 120g. (little) - warm - acrid ....metal
Tomato 2 pieces (blended) / 200g. (rec.) - cold - sweet-sour....................wood
Olive oil 2 table spoons / 20g. (little) - cool - sweet ....earth
Salt 1 pinch / 0,5g. (little) - cold - salty ....water
Parsley 1 table spoon (chopped) / 8g. (rec.) - warm - bitter ....wood
Thyme 1/2 teaspoon / 1g. (little) - warm - bitter.. *
Onion (spring) 2 table spoons (chopped) / 12g. (little) - warm - acrid........metal
Basil 4 leaves / 2g. (yes) - warm - acrid, bitter ....fire

Cooking instructions:

Use double the amount of water to polenta, add salt and oil and heat till it boils. Stir in polenta, stirring constantly. Take off the fire and let it swell for 20 minutes. Meanwhile, cut the onion, fry in a saucepan with hot oil. Add the diced zucchini, tomatoes and melanzani and simmer for about 20 minutes. Add basil, thyme, salt.
Coat baking tray with oil, apply polenta evenly and wait until it gets stronger.
Add the cooked ratatouille to polenta, portion and then put in the oven for a few minutes (possibly with grated parmesan).
Sprinkle with fresh parsley and finely chopped spring onion.
The valuable tip: The Polenta sections are ideal for on the go.

9.17 Pumpkin soup

Forces lungs and spleen, diuretic, forces Qi, protects liver, forces Qi, forces spleen, relieves inflammation, moisturizes, relaxes, builds up Qi, spreads, strengthens spleen and liver, regulates Qi flow, moisturizes, relaxes, builds up Qi, spreads.
Cooking time approx. 1 hour
Calories p. portion: 105
3 portions

Quantity of ingredients:

Pumpkin 3/4 lbs / 300g. (yes) - warm - sweet ....earth
Carrot 2 pieces / 100g. (yes) - neutral - sweet ....earth
Potato 2 pieces / 120g. (yes) - neutral - sweet...earth
Olive oil 1 table spoon / 10g. (little) - cool - sweet.....................................earth
Onion white 1 piece / 50g. (little) - warm - acrid ....metal
Water 1 cup / 120g. (yes) - cool - salty..earth
Parsley 1 table spoon / 7g. (rec.) - warm - bitter ....wood

Anise (Common Fennel) 1 pinch / 1g. (little) - warm - acrid ....earth
Salt 1 pinch / 1g. (little) - cold - salty ....water

Cooking instructions:
Add the olive oil to the pan, add the diced pumpkin, diced carrots and potatoes. Roast them shortly, add the finely chopped onion, fill with water, add enough water to cover the vegetables at least 3 finger-widths. Boil at low heat.

Season with sea salt, add small cutted parsley, a pinch of anise (little). Allow to simmer for about 35 minutes. Then purée the soup and add some water, depending on the consistency of the soup.

9.18 Quick zucchini soup

Reduces mucus, preserves the fluids, cools liver fire, forces stomach Qi.
Cooking time approx. 10 min
Calories p. portion: 42
4 portions

Quantity of ingredients:
Zucchini 2-3 pieces / 500g. (yes) - cool - sweet ....earth
Onion white 1 piece / 50g. (little) - warm - acrid ....metal
Corn germ oil 2 table spoons / 6g. (yes) - neutral - sweet.........................earth
Parsley 1 table spoon / 7g. (rec.) - warm - bitter ....wood
Chives 1 teaspoon / 3g. (little) - warm - acrid ....metal
Water 2 cup / 400g. (yes) - cool - salty..earth

Cooking instructions:
Fry chopped onion in oil. Add sliced zucchini and sauté well. Pour with water. Chop parsley and chives, add and puree everything.

9.19 Rice congee with honey pear and black sesame

Especially good in kidney Yin deficiency, moisturizes lungs, cools heat, reduces lung mucus, produces humors, moisturizes, relaxes, builds up Qi, spreads, moisturizes intestines, nourishes Yin.
Cooking time approx. 10 min - 3 hours
Calories p. portion: 158
2 portions
Allergens: N

Quantity of ingredients:
Basic recipe … (Congee) 1 1/2 cups / 240g. (yes) - neutral - sweet .... *
Pear 2 pieces / 300g. (yes) - cool - sweet, sour ....earth
Sesame, black1 teaspoon / 3g. (little) - cool.. metal

Cooking instructions:
Cook rice congee according to basic recipe.
Fill pot with 3 cm of water and heat till it boils. Quarter the pears (with
the skin and seeds) and simmer them covered with black sesame for 10
minutes. Mix with the rice.

9.20 Roasted millet with Celery sticks

Strengthens spleen and kidney, diuretic, brings the liver Qi in motion,
cools heat, moisturizes, relaxes, builds up Qi, spreads.
Cooking time approx. 30 min
Calories p. portion: 400
2 portions
Allergens: L

Quantity of ingredients:
Millet 1 cup / 120g. (rec.) - cool - sweet, salty ....earth
Water 1 1/2 cups / 240g. (yes) - cool - salty..earth
Celery sticks 2 rods / 50g. (yes) - cool - sweet...earth
Water 2 table spoons / 30g. (yes) - cool - salty ....earth
Salt 1 pinch / 1g. (little) - cold - salty .... water
Sage 3-4 leaves / 2g. (yes) - cool - bitter, spicy ....fire
Cress 1 teaspoon / 3g. (yes) - cool - sweet... metal

Cooking instructions:
Roast millet briefly, pour over water, heat till it boils and let stand for 20
min. to swell.
Cut celery into small pieces and mix with water, salt and fresh herbs
and cook for 10 min. Add to the millet. Sprinkle fresh sage or
watercress over it.

9.21 Roasted nuts

Strengthens kidney Qi, essence and brain, forces kidney, builds up
essence, warms lungs, moistens the intestine, moisturizes, relaxes,
builds up Qi, spreads.
Cooking time approx. 5 min
Calories p. portion: 973
2 portions
Allergens: H

Quantity of ingredients:
Hazelnuts 10 cups / 100g. (rec.) - neutral - sweet.....................................earth
Cashews 10 cups / 100g. (yes) - cool - sweet..earth
Walnuts 1/4 lbs - 4oz / 100g. (rec.) - warm - sweet ....earth

Cooking instructions:
Roast nuts in a pan for about 5 minutes.

9.22 Rucola salad with tomatoes

Refreshing, builds up blood and fluids, nourishes liver-Yin, cools heat, produces humors, gets Qi moving, reduces internal heat.
Cooking time approx. 10 min
Calories p. portion: 129
1 portion
Allergens: O

Quantity of ingredients:
Olive oil 1 table spoon / 10g. (little) - cool - sweet.....................................earth
Pepper (ground) 1 pinch / 0,2g. () - warm - acrid ....metal
Salt 1 pinch / 0,3g. (little) - cold - salty ....water
Vinegar (Apple vinegar) 1 dash / 1g. (little) - warm - sour, bitter ....wood
Tomato 4 pieces / 200g. (rec.) - cold - sweet-sour...................................wood
Rucola 2 handful / 30g. () - cool - acrid ....fire

Cooking instructions:
In a salad bowl stir in olive oil, freshly ground pepper, salt, vinegar and diced tomatoes; plenty of finely shredded rucola leaves.
Variants: Cut shiitake mushrooms into fine strips: Fry one half in a little butter and mix with the other half of raw shiitake under the salad. In place of shiitake mushrooms can be used.
Serve with: toasted bread, polenta.

9.23 Russian kasha with white cabbage

Strengthens spleen stomach and intestine Qi, has a slightly warming effect.
Cooking time approx. 30 min
Calories p. portion: 250
2 portions
Allergens: AG

Quantity of ingredients:
Buckwheat whole grain 1 cup / 130g. (yes) - cool - sweet......................... wood
Water 1 1/2 cups / 240g. (yes) - cool - salty ....earth
Nutmeg 1 pinch / 1g. (little) - warm - acrid.. metal
Salt 1 pinch / 1g. (little) - cold - salty .... water
Parsley 1 table spoon / 10g. (rec.) - warm - bitter .... wood
Ground 1 pinch / 2g. (little) - warm - acrid .... metal
Butter organic 1 teaspoon / 3g. (yes) - neutral - sweet..............................earth
White cabbage 1 handful / 20g. (yes) - neutral - sweet ....earth

Cooking instructions:
Roast buckwheat golden yellow; add boiling water, heat till it boils briefly and then let it swell until soft; Grate the white cabbage finely and fold in. Season with nutmeg, a little salt; some parsley, cumin and butter at the end.

9.24 Summer Salad

Nourishes liver-Yin, cools heat, dissolves mucus, forces Xu-conditions, passes downwardly, brings blood into motion.
Cooking time approx. 10 min
Calories p. portion: 281
1 portion
Allergens: GMNO

Quantity of ingredients:
Rucola 1 handful / 15g. () - cool - acrid ....fire
Radicchio 1 head / 30g. (rec.) - cool - sweet, acrid, bitter ....fire
Tomato 15 pieces (diced) / 100g. (rec.) - cold - sweet-sour .... wood
Olive oil 1 table spoon / 10g. (little) - cool - sweet....................................earth
Olives 2 table spoons / 16g. (yes) - neutral - sweet, rough ....fire
Vinegar Aceto Balsamico 1 table spoon / 10g. (little) - warm - sour, bitter wood
Salt 1 pinch / 0,5g. (little) - cold - salty .... water
Pepper (ground) 1 pinch / 0,2g. () - warm - acrid .... metal
Rosemary 2 teaspoons / 3g. (little) - warm - bitter...fire

Cooking instructions:
Wash the salad, pluck it small and arrange it in a bowl.

Sauce: Put the oil, the balsamic vinegar, the mustard and the tahini in a glass with a lid and shake well. Season the dressing with salt and pepper. Mix the salad with the salad dressing and the olives, sprinkle with parmesan and finally with rosemary.

9.25 Tea from chamomile

Reduces internal wind and heat, cools liver.
Cooking time approx. 10 min
Calories p. portion: 0
1 portion

Quantity of ingredients:
Chamomile 1 teaspoon / 3g. (rec.) - cool - sweet, bitter .... *
Water 1 cup / 120g. (yes) - cool - salty ....earth

Cooking instructions:
Heat the water till it boils and put it aside. Chamomile flowers added
and 10 min. to let go.

9.26 Tea from coriander

Sudorific, reduces wind.
Cooking time approx. 10 min
Calories p. portion: 2
4 portions

Quantity of ingredients:
Coriander 1 teaspoon / 3g. (rec.) - warm - acrid.. metal
Water 2 cup / 500g. (yes) - cool - salty ....earth

Cooking instructions:
Heat the water till it boils and put it aside. Add coriander and 10 min. to
let go. Sweet to taste with honey. Strain when pouring.

9.27 Tea from passion blossoms

Forces liver-Qi.
Cooking time approx. 10 min
Calories p. portion: 0
4 portions

Quantity of ingredients:
Water 2 cup / 500g. (yes) - cool - salty ....earth
Passion blossoms 1 teaspoon / 3g. (rec.) .... *

Cooking instructions:
Heat the water till it boils and put it aside. Add passion flower tea and let
it rest for 10 min. to let go. Strain. Sweet to taste with honey.

9.28 Tomato with mozzarella

Nourishes liver-Yin, cools heat, produces humors.
Cooking time approx. 5 min
Calories p. portion: 436
1 portion
Allergens: AG

Quantity of ingredients:
Mozzarella 1 piece / 50g. (yes) - neutral - sweet...earth
Tomato 2 pieces / 100g. (rec.) - cold - sweet-sour ....wood
Salt 1 pinch / 1g. (little) - cold - salty ....water
Basil (fresh) 5 leaves / 6g. (omit) - warm - acrid, bitter..............................metal
Olive oil 2 table spoons / 20g. (little) - cool - sweet ....earth
White bread (wheat bread) 2 slices / 40g. (yes) - cool - sweet..................wood

Cooking instructions:
Cut tomatoes and mozzarella into slices. Serve with salt, basil and olive oil. Serve with white bread.

9.29 Vegetable bowl with Provencal pistou

Strengthens spleen and liver, regulates Qi flow, relaxes, builds up Qi, spreads, dries out, passes downwardly, strengthens stomach Qi, regulates Qi, warms the inside, lowers cold, forces stomach, relieves constipation.
Cooking time approx. 1 1/2 hours
Calories p. portion: 138
8 portions
Allergens: AGL

Quantity of ingredients:
Tomato 5/8 oz / 200g. (rec.) - cold - sweet-sour.. wood
Olive oil 2 table spoons / 30g. (little) - cool - sweet ....earth
Garlic 1 clove / 5g. (omit) - hot - acrid .... metal
Basil (fresh) 1 Bunch / 125g. (omit) - warm - acrid, bitter .... metal
Salt 1 pinch / 2g. (little) - cold - salty ....water
Pepper (ground) 1 pinch / 1g. () - warm - acrid .... metal
Oregano dried 1 teaspoon / 3g. (little) - warm - bitter................................ metal
Basic recipe for a vegetable soup (nutritious) 3 lbs / 1250g. (yes) - neutral - * *
Carrot 3/8 lbs - 6oz / 150g. (yes) - neutral - sweet ....earth
Celery root 1/4 lbs - 4oz / 100g. (rec.) - cool - sweet.................................earth
Broccoli 5/8 oz / 200g. (yes) - cool - sweet...earth
Fennel 1 piece / 250g. (yes) - warm - sweet, little acrid ....earth
Thyme dried 1/2 teaspoon / 2g. (omit) - warm - bitter .... metal
Oregano dried 1/2 teaspoon / 2g. (little) - warm - bitter.............................. metal

Bay leaf 1 piece / 0,5g. (little) - warm - acrid .... metal
Peas, green 1/8 lbs - 2oz / 50g. (yes) - neutral - sweet .... water
Onion (spring onion) 4 pieces / 80g. (little) - warm - acrid .... metal
Potato 1/4 lbs - 4oz / 100g. (yes) - neutral - sweet .... earth

Cooking instructions:

Sauce:
Tear off tomatoes and cut into small pieces. Reduce in a pot with a little olive oil, finely chopped garlic. Add 1 slice of
dry toasted bread (crumbed), fresh finely grated Parmesan, finely chopped basil, oregano, salt and pepper.

Soup:
Boil the vegetable broth according to the basic recipe, add coarsely sliced carrots, diced celery, diced potatoes, small florets, broccoli, finely chopped fennel tuber, peas, thyme, oregano and the bay leaf. let cook 10 minutes.

Cut 4 scallions into thin rings, add them and cook another 2 min.

Pour sauce into a soup bowl. First only a few tablespoons. Stir boiling broth with it, then stir in the soup little by little.

9.30 Vegetable rice

Strengthens spleen and liver, regulates Qi flow, relaxes, builds up Qi, spreads, dries out, passes downwardly, strengthens stomach Qi, warms the stomach and spleen, harmonizes the intestine, forces Qi, reduces moisture.
Cooking time approx. 30 min
Calories p. portion: 304
3 portions
Allergens: L

Quantity of ingredients:

Broccoli 1/8 lbs - 2oz / 50g. (yes) - cool - sweet .... earth
Carrot 1/8 lbs - 2oz / 50g. (yes) - neutral - sweet .... earth
Kohlrabi 1/8 lbs - 2oz / 50g. (little) - neutral - acrid, sweet .... earth
Cauliflower 1 oz / 30g. (yes) - cool - sweet .... earth
Peas 1/2 oz / 20g. (yes) - neutral - sweet, salty .... water
Margarine 1 teaspoon / 4g. (little) - cool - sweet .... earth
Rice (whole grain) 5/8 oz / 200g. (yes) - warm - sweet .... metal
Basic recipe for a vegetable soup (nutritious) 7/8 lbs / 400g. (yes) - neutral - **
Parsley 1/2 oz / 20g. (rec.) - warm - bitter .... wood
Pepper (ground) 1 pinch / 0,2g. () - warm - acrid .... metal

Cooking instructions:
Cut the broccoli, carrots and kohlrabi into small cubes, divide the cauliflower into small florets. Heat the margarine in a pan or saucepan, sauté the vegetables. Then add the rice, top up with the vegetable stock and leave to soak for 15-20 minutes.

In the meantime, finely chop the parsley. After cooking, season the rice with freshly ground pepper and parsley.

9.31 Wheat fresh grain porridge with pears.

Moisturizes lungs, cools heat, reduces lung mucus, nourishes Yin from heart and kidney, forces heart and kidney, moisturizes, relaxes, builds up Qi, spreads.
Cooking time approx. 25 min
Calories p. portion: 309
2 portions
Allergens: ANO

Quantity of ingredients:
Wheat 1 cup / 100g. (yes) - cool - sweet.. wood
Water 2-4 cups / 350g. (yes) - cool - salty...earth
Pear 2 pieces / 300g. (yes) - cool - sweet, sour ....earth
Raisins 1 table spoon / 10g. (yes) - warm - sweet.....................................earth
Sesame, white 1 table spoon / 8g. (rec.) - neutral - sweet ....earth
Sunflower seeds 1 table spoon / 8g. (rec.) - neutral - sweet ....earth
Cardamom 1 pinch / 0,3g. () - warm - acrid... metal
Salt 1 pinch / 0,3g. (little) - cold - salty .... water

Cooking instructions:
Preparation the night before: Wheat roughly cut; soak overnight.

In the morning: Put the wheat meal with a little hot water; simmer with stirring for about 15 minutes.
Meanwhile, add pear compote, raisins, crushed sesame, sunflower seeds, some ground cardamom, a small pinch of salt.

Variants: with grated apple or seasonal fruit.

10 Effects of food

10.1 Use ingredients: recommendable

Aubergine
Barley
Barley flour
Barley not peeled
Basic recipe for a chicken soup
(warming)
Beef heart
Beef liver
Blackberry jam
Blackberry´s
Blueberry
Blueberry jam
Blueberry juice
Calamari
Celery root
Chamomile
Chard
Cherry
Chicken liver
Chicken meat
Chicken yolk
Chicory
Chlorella (fresh water)
Coriander
Duck (slaughtered)
Eel
Freshwater fish
Grape juice red
Grapes red
Grass carp
Hazelnuts
Kaki plum
Lamb liver
Leaf salads (bitter)
Lemon
Lemon juice
Loquate / Japanese medlar
Lychee

Millet
Millet flakes
Mulberry fruit
Nasturtium (nose-twister or nose-tweaker)
Octopus
Parsley
Parsley root
Passion blossoms tea
Pearl barley
Peppermint
Perch
Plums
Quinoa
Rabbit liver
Radicchio
Raspberry
Red beet
Red berry (without sugar)
Red wine
Rice long grain rice
Rice sweet
Rose blossom tea
Sake
Sesame paste (Tahini)
Sesame, black
Sesame, white
Shrimp
Soybeans, black
Spinach
Sunflower seeds
Tomato
Tsampa (roasted barley flour)
Turkey breast meat
Walnuts
Walnuts roasted
Wheatgrass powder

10.2 Use ingredients: yes

Adzuki beans
Agave nectar
Agrimony
Almond
Almond marzipan
Almond milk
Almond puree
Apple (sweet)

Apple juice (natural cloudy)
Apple puree
Apricot
Apricots
Apricots juice
Arrowroot
Artichoke
Banana

Banana (cooking banana)
Barley grass powder
Barley grouts
Barley malt
Basic recipe for a beef soup (warming)
Basic recipe for a rice soup (Congee)
Basic recipe for a vegetable soup (nutritious)
Basil
Beans (green, fresh)
Bearberry leaf
Beef bone marrow
Beef fillet
Beef heart (calf)
Beef kidney
Beef lungs (calf)
Beef meat
Beef meat (calf)
Beef meatbones
Beef Oxtail pieces
Beef soup meat
Bitter melon
Black beans
Black fungus mushroom
Blackberry dried (unripe fruit)
Blackberry leaves
Blueberry dried
Bocksdorn fruits (Fructus Lycii, goji berry dried
Boletus mushroom
Borage oil
Bread roll
Bread with carob kernel flour
Breadcrumbs (wheat bread, bread roll)
Broad beans (thick beans)
Broccoli
Buckwheat
Buckwheat (roasted) Kasha
Buckwheat whole grain
Bush beans
Butter (half fat)
Butter beans white
Butter organic
Camembert
Carob flour, St. john's bread
Carp
Carrot
Carrot (Early Carrot)
Carrot juice without sugar
Cashews
Cauliflower
Celery sticks
Champignon
Chanterelle

Cherry (sour)
Cherry compote
Chestnuts
Chicken egg white
Chicken heart
Chicken stomach
Chickpeas
Chinese cabbage
Chrysanthemum blossom tea
Clementine
Coconut flakes
Coconut grated
Coconut milk
Coix (seeds) YiYi Ren
Corn
Corn (fast polenta)
Corn (roasted)
Corn flour
Corn germ oil
Corn Grease (Polenta)
Corn starch
Cow's milk (1.5% fat)
Cow's milk (whole milk 3.5% fat)
Cranberries
Cranberry
Cranberry jam
Cress
Cucumber (spicy cucumber)
Dates dried
Dates red
Duck (heart)
Ducks egg
Eel smoked
Elderberries
Elderberry blossom tee
Evening primrose oil
Fennel
Fennel seeds ground
Feta cheese
Fig
Fig dried
Fish pieces mixed (fresh water)
French beans
Fresh cheese from soya
Freshwater crab
Ginkgo fruit
Ginseng root
Goose
Goose egg
Goose parts
Gourd
Grape juice white
Grapefruit dried peel
Grapes white

Grapeseed oil
Herbs different varieties
Herbs various
Herbs wild
Hibiscus tea
Hijiki
Horehound leaves
Horse meat
Jasmine blossoms tee
Kidney beans (red)
King Solomon's-seal
Lemon Balm (dried)
Lemon Balm (fresh)
Lemon peel
Lentils black
Lentils red
Licorice root tea
Lime blossom tea
Linseed oil
Longane
Lotus roots
Lotus seeds
Luo Han Guo fruit
Lychee in Preserved
Malt
Manioc flour
Maple syrup
Miso
Morel (black, dried)
Morel, dried
Mozzarella
Mu Erh Mushroom
Mung bean
Mung bean sprouting
Nettles
Noodles (wheat) with egg
Noodles (wheat, lasagne) with egg
Noodles (wheat, ribbon noodles) with egg
Noodles (wheat, spaghetti) with egg
Noodles (whole grain) with egg
Okra
Olives
Olives green
Orange blossom
Orange dried peel
Orange grated peel
Orange jam
Orange peel
Oyster mushroom
Oyster shell powder
Oysters
Parmesan
Parsnip

Peanut (roasted)
Peanut butter
Peanut oil
Peanuts
Pear
Pearl barley
Peas
Peas, green
Peppers
Pig blood
Pigeon
Pine nuts
Pinto beans speckled
Pistachios
Pork brain
Pork ham cooked
Pork heart
Pork knuckle
Pork liver
Pork marrow bones
Pork meat
Pork skin
Pork stomach
Pork's intestine
Potato
Potato (mealy)
Potato flour
Pudding powder vanilla
Pumpkin
Pumpkin seeds
Quail
Quail egg
Quince
Rabbit
Rabbit (wild)
Radish
Radish black
Raisins
Raspberry jam
Raspberry leaf tea
Red cabbage
Reishi mushroom
Rice (fragrance)
Rice (Gaoliang / Sorghum)
Rice (whole grain)
Rice Basmati
Rice black
Rice flour
Rice malt
Rice mash
Rice noodles
Rice red
Rice round grain
Rice starch

Rice sticky
Rice variety any
Rice wild (nature rice)
Rooibos tea
Rye
Rye flour
Rye wholemeal bread
Saffron
Sage
Sago (cereals)
Salsify
Savoy cabbage / kale
Sea buckthorn
Sesame oil
Sesame oil roasted
Shiitake, dried
Soy cream
Soy flour
Soy noodles
Soy Tofu
Soy Tofu smoked
Soya Cuisine (soy cream)
Soybean milk
Soybeans
Soybeans, blacks, fermented
Soybeans, yellow
Stevia (candyleaf, sweetleaf)
Sugar molasses
Sugar substitute (sweetener)
Sweet potato
Trout
Truffle
Turkey ham
Turnip
Turnips
Valerian

Vanilla
Vanilla pod
Vanilla powder
Vanilla sugar natural
Vegetable juice
Water
Water hot
Wheat
Wheat bran
Wheat bulgur
Wheat flakes
Wheat flatbread/pita bread
Wheat flour
Wheat flour whole grain
Wheat semolina
Wheat semolina for children
Wheat/Rye/Gray-black bread with yeast
Wheatgrass juice
White beans
White bread (baguette)
White bread (pretzel sticks)
White bread (roll)
White bread (wheat bread)
White breadcrumbs
White cabbage
White dumpling bread (wheat bread cut into chunks)
White wine
Whitefish
Wild herbs
Wild strawberries
Wormwood herb
Yam root, yam root tuber
Yarrow
Yeast
Yew nut

10.3 Use ingredients: little

Agar agar (kelp)
Aloe juice
Angelica root
Anise (Common Fennel)
Apple (sour)
Apricot jam
Apricot nectar
Baking powder
Balm
Batavia
Bay leaf
Bean oil
Beef stomach
Beer (alcohol-free)

Beer (alcohol-reduced)
Beer (Pils)
Beer (Top-fermented German dark beer)
Berries of the season
Berry juice
Bitter Lemon
Black caraway
Black-eyed peas
Borage
Brie cheese
Brown ale
Bulgur (cereals)
Buttermilk

Caviar
Cherry juice
Chervil
Chervil dried
Chicken egg
Chinese pearl barley
Chives
Clarified butter
Clementines
Clove
Coconut fat
Coconut meat
Cooking oil
Corn silk tea
Cottage cheese
Couscous
Cranberry
Cranberry juice
Cream 10% coffee cream
Cream sour 10%
Cream sour 20%
Cream sour 30%
Cream, sweet 30%
Creamer
Crème fraiche cheese
Crispbread
Cumin (Caraway seed)
Curd cheese 20%
Curd cheese 40%
Currant (black)
Currant (red)
Currant (white)
Currant jam (black)
Currant jam (red)
Currant juice (black)
Currants (black)
Currants (red)
Deer meat
Deer meat
Deer's kidneys
Dill
Dulse (seaweed)
Dyer's broom herb
Edam cheese
Emmental cheese
Endive salad
Fennel tea
Fish innards
Fish remains
Fish sauce
Fresh cheese
Fresh cheese with herbs
Fructose (glucose)
Fruit mix juice

Gelatin white
Gentian root
Ginger fresh
Ginger oil
Goose fat
Gooseberry
Gorgonzola
Gouda cheese
Green spelt
Greengage
Ground
Ground caraway
Guava
Hawthorn
Herbs of Provence
Hibiscus
Hokkaido pumpkin
Hop
Iceberg lettuce
Kefir
Kohlrabi
Kombu seaweed (Saccharina japonica)
Kumquats
Lamb's lettuce
Lamb's lettuce
Leek
Lentils
Lentils yellow
Lettuce
Lima beans
Linseed
Linseed (crushed)
Lobster
Lychee liqueur
Lye roll
Mallow (Malva sylvestris) blossom tea
Mango juice
Margarine
Margarine (diet)
Marjoram
Mayonnaise 50%
Mineral water
Mirabelle plum
Miso black (fermented)
Miso paste (soy bean paste)
Muesli
Mulled Wine Spice
Multi-grain bread (gray bread)
Mustard
Mustard Dijon
Mustard medium hot
Mustard seeds
Mustard sweet
Nectarine

Nori, purple seaweed, red algae
Nutmeg
Oat
Oat flakes (whole grain)
Oat flakes roasted
Oat flour
Oat fusion (baby food)
Oat meal
Oat milk
Olive oil
Onion (shallot)
Onion (spring onion)
Onion read
Onion white
Orange
Oregano dried
Oregano fresh
Peaches
Peaches (canned)
Pear juice
Peppermint tea
Pheasant
Pomegranate
Pork Bacon
Pork fat (lard)
Pork ham
Pork ham smoked
Pork kidneys
Pork Lard
Pork lung
Pork sausage (Bratwurst) Pork/beef sausage (smoked)
Processed cheese 12%
Psyllium seed
Puff pastry
Pumpernickel (dark bread)
Pumpkin seed oil
Rabbit meat
Radish leaves
Rapeseed oil
Raspberry dried (immature)
Romaine lettuce / lettuce salad
Rose hip
Rose hip tea
Rosemary
Rusk
Salt
Salt (herbal)
Sauerkraut (cutted cabbage fermented)

Savory
Shrimps
Skim milk powder
Sour cherries
Sour cream (Schmand) 30% fat
Sour cream 15% fat
Sour milk
Sour milk cheese 20%
Sourdough
Soy sauce
Soybean oil
Spelled (Dark) bread
Spelled flakes
Spelled grain
Spelled semolina
Spelled wholemeal flour
Spiny lobsters
Star anise
Strawberries
Strawberry jam
Strawberry Juice
Sugar - icing sugar
Sugar brown
Sugar palm sugar
Sunflower oil
Tabasco
Tangerine
Tarragon (Estragon)
Thistle oil
Thyme
Toast bread (whole grain)
Trout (smoked)
Umeboshi plums (Japanese apricots)
Vinegar (Apple vinegar)
Vinegar (Red wine vinegar)
Vinegar Aceto Balsamico
Vinegar Aceto Balsamico white
Wakame
Walnut oil
Wax gourd
Wheat beer
Wheat germ oil
Whey
Whole grain bread
Wholemeal bread with whole grains
Wholemeal flour
Wild boar meat
Wild garlic (garlic spinach)

10.4 Do not use contra-acting foods

Amaranth
Amaranth Pops

Anchovy / Sardine
Apricot dried

Asparagus (green or white)
Avocado
Bamboo shoots
Basic recipe for a duck soup
Basic recipe for a fish soup
Basil (fresh)
Bitter liqueur
Black tea
Boxhorn clover seeds
Brussels sprouts
Burdock root tea
Campari
Cantaloupe
Capers in olive oil
Carambola (Star fruit)
Cereal coffee
Chicken Blood
Chili (pod or ground)
Chocolate
Chocolate (Diabetic)
Cinnamon ground
Cinnamon sticks
Cocoa
Cod
Codfish
Coffee
Cola drink
Cola drink (low calorie)
Coriander (fresh)
Crab
Cream (30% fat)
Crucian
Cucumber
Curry
Curry paste red
Dandelion (young plants)
Dandelion juice
Dandelionroots tea
Deer's Bones
Fernet Branca (herbal bitter liqueur)
Feta cheese
Flounder
Fruit tea
Gail plum
Garlic
Ginger powder
Ginseng liqueur
Goat
Goat and sheep's milk
Goat cheese
Grapefruit (Pomelo)
Grapefruit juice
Green tea
Halibut (Flatfish)

Herbal tea mix
Herbs bitter
Herring
Honey
Honey wine (Met)
Hyssop
Juniper berry
Kiwi
Kudzu
Ladyfingers
Lady's mantle
Lamb bones
Lamb kidneys
Lamb meat
Lamb shoulder
Lavender blossoms
Lime
Lovage
Lovage seeds
Mackerel
Mango
mango powder
Martini
Mayonnaise 80%
Mediterranean fish (cod, plaice, haddock, sea Mixed Pickles
Mold cheese
Mullet
Mussels
Mutton
Mutton
Octopus
Orange juice
Palm oil
Papaya
Pepper Cayenne
Pepper powder (hot)
Pepper white (ground)
Peppercorns
Pepperoni
Pepperoni, red, pitted, halved
Pepperoni, yellow, pitted, halved
Peppers (rose peppers)
Peppers (sweet)
Peppers powder
Pickle
Pimento
Pineapple
Pineapple (from a can)
Pineapple juice without sugar
Plaice
Plum
Plum dried
Poppy

processed cheese 30%
Prosecco
Radish (white, green, purple-red)
Radish horseradish
Rhubarb
Rosefish
Rum
Salmon
Sea cucumber
Seacrab
Shark
Sheep's milk
Sheep's milk yoghurt
Sherry (whine)
Sorrel
Spirit
Spurdog (spiny dogfish, Schillerlocken)
St. Benedict's thistle, blessed thistle,
holy thistle, Sugar candy white

Sugar cane sugar
Sugar fructose - fruit sugar
Sugar glucose - grapes sugar
Sugar Milk Sugar
Sugar white
Thyme dried
Tomato dried
Tomato juice
Tomato paste
Tomato puree
Tuna
Turmeric (yellow root)
Watermelon
Wormwood
Yarrow tea
Yoghurt vanilla
Yogi tea
Yogurt (natural, 1.5% fat)
Yogurt (natural, 3.5% fat)

11 Complementary

11.1 Chamomile

Chamaemelum nobile
Preparation: Healing tea (infusion)
Regulates liver-Qi, triggers stagnation, lowers liver-yang and internal wind, regulates lung-qi, induces hot-mucus from the lungs, evokes wind-heat and moisture-heat. Cooling.
Active ingredients: essential. Oil: chamazulen, bisabolol, flavonoids, coumarins
Dosage: Pour 2 teaspoons of the tea into 250 ml of boiling water and leave for 10 minutes. Then sieve. Drink 2 to 3 cups per day as needed.
Note: Continuous use is not recommended, otherwise harmless.

11.2 Ginger fresh

Zingiberis officinalis, Rhizoma
Preparation: Decoction
Strengthens juices production, reduces cold-nuisance, stimulates, stimulates the Yang-energy, warms the lung- and stomach-energy.
To improve the taste use brown raw sugar
Special features: In TCM, the fresh ginger root is mainly used against fish poisoning and colds of the lungs and stomach. Because ginger promotes nutrient uptake, it is often used in a variety of formulations to facilitate the rapid absorption of other

herbs and thereby enhance their effects. Ginger contains the digestive enzyme zingibain. The digestive effect of this substance is stronger than that of the enzyme papain.

Dosage: Put 1-6 slices of fresh root in a jug of water for 3 minutes. Drink 10 g in two doses on empty stomach.

Note: In too large quantities, ginger leads to constipation. Not to use in: pregnancy, high fever.

11.3 Lime/linden blossoms

Tilia cordata

Preparation: Decoction

Softens wind, lowers ascending liver-yang, moves liver-qi, stimulates diuresis, strengthens WEI QI.

Dosage: Pour 9-15 g into 250 ml of boiling water and leave for 10 minutes. Then sieve. Drink 2 to 3 cups per day as needed.

12 Basics of Nutrition

The basic principles of nutrition described herein are general recommendations. They are not aimed at a specific form of therapy. Recommendations concerning a therapy have priority.

12.1 Nutrition

Regular meals in a relaxed atmosphere. A warm breakfast is considered a good start into the day.
The main meals ought to be taken for lunch – supper in the early evening. Pay attention to feeling hungry or sated: don't eat too much nor remain hungry is the rule
Prepare the meals freshly from natural, regional products. Frozen, heat-conserved, industrially prepared or foodstuffs cooked in the microwave oven are rejected.
Choice of foodstuffs according to the season: more cooling food in summer, more warming food in winter.
Eat cooked food at least twice a day. Food and drinks ought to be lukewarm, never ice-cold or hot.
Raw vegetables, briefly cooked vegetables, freshly squeezed juices and mineral water are not recommended. Milk and dairy products are only included in the diet if they don't cause problems.
Don't use therapeutic recipes over a longer period without consulting your doctor or therapist.

Varied food
Enjoy the diversity of foodstuffs. Characteristics of a balanced nutrition are variety, suitable combination and a balanced quantity of rich and low energy foodstuffs (on one hand avoiding undersupply with essential nutrients and on the other hand to take to many undesirable substances).

A lot of Cereal Products - and Potatoes
Bread, pasta, rice, cereal flakes (best wholemeal) as well as potatoes contain almost no fat, but many vitamins, mineral nutrients, trace elements, roughage and secondary plant substances. These foodstuffs ought to be taken with low-fat side dishes.

Vegetables and Fruit – „Take Five" every day ...
5 portions of vegetables and fruit a day, as fresh as possible, briefly cooked, or maybe one portion as a juice – ideal as a side dish to every meal as well as snack between meals: Thus a lot of vitamins, mineral nutrients as well as roughage and secondary plant substances

Daily milk and dairy products
Milk and Dairy Products every Day, once or twice per Week Fish; meat, sausages as well as eggs moderately. These foodstuffs contain valuable nutrients like calcium in the milk, iodine selenium and omega-3 fat acids in saltwater fish. Meat is favorable due to its high content of disposable iron and the vitamins B1, B6 and B12. Quantities of 300 – 600 g meat and sausage per week are sufficient. Prefer low-fat products, especially in meat- and dairy products.

Low-fat and fatty Foodstuffs
Fat supplies us with essential fat acids and fatty foodstuffs contain also fat-soluble vitamins. Fat is high in energy; therefore much fat in the food may cause overweight, possibly also cancer. Too many saturated fat acids may further a tendency for cardio-vascular diseases in the long term. Prefer vegetable oils and fats (e.g. rapeseed-, olive-, soya-oils and solid fats produced therefrom). Beware of invisible fat in meat- and dairy products, pastry and sweets as well as in fast-food and convenience foods. 70 – 90 g fat per day is sufficient.

Moderately Sugar and Salt
Take sugar and foods/drinks containing various kinds of sugar (e.g. glucose syrup) only occasionally. Use herbs and spices as well as a little salt creatively. Prefer salt containing iodine.

Plenty of Liquids
Water is absolutely essential. Drink 1-2 l liquids every day. Prefer water (with or without gas) and other low-calorie drinks. Alcoholic drinks should not be taken.

Tasty Dishes, carefully cooked
Cook the meals with as low temperatures and as short as possible, using little water and fat – this preserves the original taste, keeps the nutrients intact and prevents the production of harmful compounds.

Take time and enjoy the food
Take your Time and enjoy your Food
Eating consciously helps to eat right. The eye enjoys food, too. It's fun, invites to enjoy varied dishes and stimulates the feeling of satiety.

Watch your Weight and stay in Motion
A balanced diet and a lot of exercise and sport (30 – 60 min/day) are a healthy combination. The right weight furthers well-being and health. Thermals, directional effectiveness, digestive power

There are various criteria for judging the effectiveness of herbs and foodstuffs.

The use of certain herbs and ingredients is based on observations of the effects on the body which these foodstuffs, herbs and spices show after having eaten them. The medical science has developed following system: Every ingredient or herb has a directional effectiveness. Furthermore, there are herbs which have a special effect on certain organs.

The basic condition for a healthy metabolism is to obtain sufficient energy from food and that the digestive process doesn't use too much energy. An easily digestible meal makes content and sated, doesn't cause flatulence and fatigue after the meal. The perfect spices increase the healthiness of our meals. Very often, just small doses of herbs and spices will suffice. They are not used to make us sated, but to help our digestive organs to digest the food.

12.2 Recipes

The recipes list the ingredients to be used and the cooking instructions show how the dish is prepared. The list of ingredients shows the concerned quantities as well as the relevance for the therapy. If you find „less than mentioned", try to comply or find an alternative from the „list of recommended foodstuffs". Mostly it shall result just in a small change of taste when you simply avoid this ingredient.

Mild cooking methods: boiling, stewing, poaching, steaming
Strong cooking methods: barbecuing, roasting, frying, smoking
Balanced cooking methods: deep-frying, baking brick
Deep-freezing and warming in the microwave oven should be avoided (denaturalization).

12.3 Foodstuffs

Foodstuffs have an effect on body and soul like medicinal herbs, only a very much milder one. Dietary advice is mainly based on regional foodstuffs. The knowledge about the effects of each foodstuff and the knowledge, when which foodstuff shall be used, is based on the orthodox school of medicine. Use ecologic-organic products, if possible. As everything should be cooked for a long time due to a better digestability and very rarely eaten raw, the food agrees with everyone.

The classification of the foodstuffs according to their effect on the body is the basis in order to achieve a harmonious status of health.

Dietary advisors do not recommend certain foodstuffs for everyone. The individual diet is tailor-made for the individual constitution.

Buy only fresh and ripe fruit and vegetables. You ought to leave unripe fruit and vegetables and such with brown spots and wilted leaves behind in the market. In this case take deep-frozen goods (never ready-to-serve dishes!). Fruit and vegetables are deep-frozen immediately after harvesting and often contain more vitamins and minerals than the goods from the vegetable shelf. Whereas conserved or tinned goods contain very much less biological substances. Also, salt, sugar and others are mostly added to the latter. Never leave the foodstuffs in the water after washing them to avoid that many vital substances get drowned. Clean salads, fruit and vegetables immediately before serving.

Please make sure of the hygienic processing of foodstuffs. Clean your salads, fruit and vegetables carefully. When cooking with meat, prepare all ingredients first and then process the meat products. Clean the worktop and tools very carefully. Wooden surfaces ought to be treated with a mild disinfectant regularly in order to reduce germination.

Store fruit and vegetables separately, if possible. Harvested fruit and vegetables are still alive and emit e.g. ethylene gas, which makes other products ripen and age faster. Keep meat and fish in the closed packaging or store them in the fridge in closed containers.

12.4 Herbs

There are some basic rules for storing medicinal herbs. On principle, herbs must be protected from direct sunlight, humidity and heat.

Containers for the storage of herbs may be glasses, ceramic jars and even plastic containers. However, plastic is a rather unsuitable material and should only be a short-term solution. In case of glass containers, use a dark material.

Medicinal herbs cannot be kept for any long period. The shelf life of herbs is limited. However, it can be prolonged with suitable storage. The place should be dark, rather cool and absolutely dry. A wooden medicine cabinet, placed not directly next to a source of heat, would be ideal. Never buy large quantities of herbs so as not to have to throw them away. Label the container with the name of the herb and the date of harvesting or processing.

13 Other dietic-books

The following syndromes of dietetics, TCM or for a therapy supplement for cancer are available.

Dietetics

E001. Nutrition of the infant - baby food
E002. Nutrition during lactation
E003. Nutrition in old age
E004. Nutrition of children and adolescents
E005. Nutrition of athletes
E006. Light weight
E007. Pregnancy
E008. Full food

Protein and electrolyte - kidneys
E009. (hemodialysis) dialysis treatment
E010. Acute renal failure
E011. Chronic renal insufficiency
E012. Nephrotic syndrome
E013. Kidney stones (nephrolithiasis)

Gastrointestinal tract - pancreas
E014. Acute pancreatitis (inflammation of the pancreas)
E015. Chronic pancreatitis (inflammation of the pancreas)

Gastrointestinal tract - small intestine and large intestine
E016. Acute obstipation (constipation)
E017. Chronic obstipation (constipation)
E018. Colon irritabile
E019. Diverticulitis
E020. Acquired lactose intolerance (lactose malabsorption)
E021. Fructose malabsorption
E022. Glutensensitive enteropathy (celiac disease)
E023. Colectomy
E024. Short Bowel Syndrome

Gastrointestinal tract - liver, gallbladder, bile ducts
E025. Acute and chronic hepatitis (inflammation of the liver)
E026. Cholelithiasis (bile stones)
E027. fatty liver
E028. cirrhosis

Gastrointestinal tract - Stomach and duodenal intestine
E029. Acute gastritis
E030. Chronic gastritis
E031. Stomach bleeding
E032. Ulcus ventriculi and duodenal ulcer
E033. Condition after gastric surgery

Gastrointestinal tract - oral cavity and esophagus
E034. Stomatitis
E035. Esophageal carcinoma (esophageal cancer)
E036. Refluosophagitis (heartburn)

Special diseases
E037. Phenylketonuria (PKU)
E038. Rheumatic joint diseases

Metabolism
E039. Obesity (overweight)
E040. Diabetes mellitus
E041. Eating disorders (underweight)

Fat metabolism
E042. Hypercholesterolaemia (increased cholesterol level)
E043. Hepatic Encephalopathy

Heart and circulation
E044. Arteriosclerosis (arterial calcification)
E045. Heart insufficiency
E046. Hypertension
E047. Hyperuricaemia and gout

Changed nutrient requirements
E048. In case of fever
E049. For malignant diseases
E050. After burns
E051. Radiation and chemotherapy

CANCER
E100. Pancreatic cancer
E101. Bladder cancer
E102. Blood cancer (leukemia)
E103. Breast cancer
E104. Colorectal cancer
E105. Gastric cancer
E106. Kidney cancer
E107. Esophageal cancer

TCM
E200. Bladder - moisture heat in the bladder
E201. Bladder - moisture and cold in the bladder
E202. Bladder - emptiness and cold in the bladder
E203. Large intestine - external cold affects the large intestine
E204. Large intestine - moisture heat in the large intestine
E205. Large intestine - heat blocks the intestine II acute
E206. Large intestine - dryness of the colon
E207. Large intestine - Yang deficiency (cold)
E208. Heart - Blood insufficiency
E209. Heart - Blood stagnation
E210. Heart - Fire
E211. Heart - Hot mucus clogs the heart pores

E212. Heart - Cold mucus clogs the heart pores
E213. Heart - Qi deficiency
E214. Heart - Yang deficiency
E215. Heart - Yin deficiency
E216. Liver - Ascending Liver Yang
E217. Liver - Blood deficiency
E218. Liver - Blood stagnation
E219. Liver - Moisture heat in liver and gall bladder
E220. Liver - Fire
E221. Liver - Gall bladder Qi-Empty
E222. Liver - Cold in the liver meridian
E223. Liver - Qi stagnation
E224. Liver - Wind
E225. Liver - Wind with ascending liver Yang
E226. Liver - Wind with blood anemic
E227. Liver - Wind with extreme heat
E228. Lung - Qi deficiency
E229. Lung - Mucus-moisture in the lungs
E230. Lung - Mucus-heat in the lungs
E231. Lung - Mucus-cold in the lungs
E232. Lung - Dryness of the lungs
E233. Lung - Wind-heat attacks the lungs
E234. Lung - Wind-cold affects the lungs
E235. Lung - Yin deficiency
E236. Stomach - Bloodstagnation
E237. Stomach - Fire
E238. Stomach - Cold with liquid
E239. Stomach - Nutrition stagnation
E240. Stomach - Qi deficiency
E241. Stomach - Rebellious Qi
E242. Stomach - Yin Emptiness
E243. Spleen - Heat and moisture attack the spleen
E244. Spleen - Coldness and moisture affects the spleen
E245. Spleen - Qi deficiency
E246. Spleen - Qi deficiency + Declining spleen Qi
E247. Spleen - Qi deficiency + spleen does not control the blood
E248. Spleen - Yang deficiency
E249. Kidney - Heart and kidney no longer communicate
E250. Kidney - Jing deficiency
E251. Kidney - Kidneys cannot receive the Qi
E252. Kidney - Qi is not stable
E253. Kidney - Yang deficiency
E254. Kidney - Yin deficiency

For further information visit di-book.com.

14 EBNS - Software for nutritional counseling

The main task of the database is to create personalized nutritional advice for each patient individually. The database was developed for Dietetics

and Traditional Chinese Medicine.
The Database supports training and advices in the daily work routine.

The computer program provides lists of recipes, ingredients and herbs, which are given to the client. individually adjustable according to patient's request from whole food to vegetarians (lacto, ovo, ...). For every register there is an information sheet which can be given to the client. All texts can be individually designed.

The syndromes can be combined and result in an intersection of the recommended recipes and ingredients. The automated diagnosis for the TCM enables you to check your experience during the training as well as to confirm your diagnosis in the working day. You select several predefined symptoms and have the program automatically display the relevant syndromes.

How to work with the database:
Select the patient / client, select one or more of the syndromes you diagnosed and print the folder.

You can change all values, create new symptoms or syndromes, develop recipes, change or adapt ingredients and herbs to your findings. In simple client management, all relevant data about the person is stored. You get an overview of the past diagnoses and the development of the course of the disease.

As a consultant you save a lot of time when you print out the recipe, food and herbal lists for the recognized syndromes and give them to the clients. You can use this time for a personal conversation. With the database, dieticians and nutritionists can view the nutrients and trace elements for each recipe and develop recipes for syndromes even with suggested ingredients.

All recipe and grocery lists can also be ordered from me as a combination of several diseases. I wish all readers good luck, health and happiness in life.
More information can be found at www.ebns.at.
Volunteer: www.krebsinfo.at
Josef Miligui